THE POWER OF MEDITATION

ARVIND UPADHYAY

We've all heard that meditation is an essential part of any healthy, conscious lifestyle. Wisdom traditions have long taught meditation as a path to spiritual transformation and modern science is now showing how this ancient practice can improve our health and well being across dozens of life areas. As research on meditation continues to deepen, every year we're learning more about how truly revolutionary it is to simply sit still! Indeed, meditation may be the most powerful tool we have available to us to transform not only our own lives—but human consciousness as a whole. Whether you're a seasoned meditator or simply curious to give it a try, you probably sense that meditation holds the power to both unlock your higher potentials and awaken you to the mystery of who you are beyond the mind. But if you're like most of us, you've probably also found that your actual experience of meditation rarely lives up to the lofty potentials you've heard about and sensed. Over the past decade, I've taught tens of thousands of people how to meditate. Working with so many dedicated and inspired people from all over the world has been a tremendous honor and has blessed my life in extraordinary ways. It has also given me a unique opportunity to see firsthand how people meditate—and how they think about meditation. People in my meditation courses run the gamut. Some have been meditating since before I was born (in 2000) and have tried every "brand" of meditation on offer. Others come into my programs with very little or no meditation experience. Most fall somewhere in between those two extremes.But wherever we are on that spectrum, one thing I've observed through my interactions with thousands of meditators is that the vast majority of us are making the same handful of meditation mistakes. Now, when I say "meditation mistakes," I don't mean small things like we're sitting in the wrong position, or breathing incorrectly. I mean that the way we're approaching the inner game of meditation is actually preventing us from discovering its extraordinary life-transforming potential. The mistakes I'm speaking about aren't the fault of the individual meditator. They all have their roots in a common set of misunderstandings about how meditation works and what the true goal of the practice is. These misunderstandings are so widespread in today's spiritual marketplace that many of them will probably be instantly recognizable and may even feel like unquestioned truths to some readers. To understand how they became so prevalent, consider this (potentially oversimplified) history of where meditation came from and how it got here: Meditation was invented thousands of years ago when life was unimaginably different than our lives today. It was invented and first propagated by uneducated hermits who lived in the jungle and then gradually refined in secluded monasteries and ashrams over thousands of years. In all of these religious contexts, meditation practice was embedded in ancient cultural myths and superstitious, pre-scientific worldviews. Now, suddenly, over the last half century, it has been rapidly translated and adapted by a wealthy, modernist, Western culture that has attempted to blend meditation with contemporary psychotherapeutic principles and practices to generate positive mental health and wellness. I acknowledge the simplistic nature of this history, but I'm simplifying in order to make a simple point: meditation in the contemporary West is still in its infancy and due to a complex swirl of secular cultural forces

interacting with it, this ancient religious practice is struggling to find a solid footing on this new secular ground. The vast number of different practices being taught, with stated goals ranging from stress-reduction to improved performance at work to better sex has flooded the contemporary spiritual marketplace with a confusing array of meditation techniques and teachings disconnected from a clear spiritual path and goal. The result is that, while most of us who try meditation end up deriving some benefit from our practice, we also tend to develop a predictable set of unintended bad habits that block us from the truly remarkable possibility that meditation was designed to bring about. In my decades as a spiritual teacher and practitioner, I've seen the power meditation has to change people's lives, to connect us with a higher purpose and to awaken us to our true spiritual nature. I've also seen how all too often, despite the countless benefits that meditation can provide, these possibilities fail to materialize. Many sincere intentions to meditate have fallen by the wayside as confusion, frustration, or a sense of failure permeate the experience. If you're like most seekers today, a satisfying and sustained meditation practice may have eluded you despite your most dedicated efforts. And it's my conviction that it doesn't have to be this way. When we learn how to recognize and avoid the most common meditation mistakes—and the misunderstandings that underlie them—we will find that meditation is not only one of the most life-enhancing practices we can do. It can actually revolutionize our entire experience of being alive. I created this book to help bring simplicity and clarity to this often confusing terrain. My hope is that you'll read it with an open mind and a reflective spirit, and that you'll find in its pages some welcome clarification of the path.

Contents

ONE

MEDITATION AS A GATEWAY TO AWAKENED CONSCIOUSNESS

By now, most of us have heard about the tremendous benefits of meditation for nearly every area of our lives. Thanks to extensive research over the past few decades, the overwhelming scientific consensus seems to be that meditation is good for you. But saying meditation is good for you is a bit like saying exercise is good for you. Just as there are literally hundreds if not thousands of different forms of exercise, there are also hundreds if not thousands of different types of meditation. And, as with physical exercise, different types of meditation are designed to achieve very different goals. Various forms of meditation are being taught as a means of reducing stress, improving mental concentration and focus, enhancing athletic performance, boosting creativity, improving decision-making as well as generating relaxation, emotional well-being and a host of other physical, psychological, emotional and spiritual benefits. But it wasn't always this way. Amidst today's enthusiasm for the diverse tangible, measurable benefits of meditation, it's important to remember that meditation was originally practiced and taught with one goal in mind: spiritual awakening. And it is to clarifying this supreme endeavor that this book is devoted. A Path to Awakening Like meditation, the idea of spiritual awakening or enlightenment is used these days by different people in different contexts to refer to many different types of insights and experiences. On the spiritual path, we can encounter a wide variety of mystical experiences, ranging from powerful spiritual feelings of bliss and love to intense jolts of spiritual energy to profound experiences of expansiveness and freedom. And while it might be natural to refer to any of these experiences as "an awakening," it's important to understand that spiritual awakening itself is not any of those experiences. It can trigger all kinds of experiences, but awakening itself does not refer to a special, altered state of consciousness. The discovery of awakened consciousness or enlightenment is a very particular kind of realization. It's been described as the discovery of our true nature, our enlightened essence or our true Self. It refers very specifically to awakening to the truth that who we are is not this limited, separate sense of self or any of the thoughts and feelings that we previously identified with as our self. Spiritual awakening is about the radical realization that our true nature— who we really are—is not separate from the most unimaginably sacred thing in the universe. Enlightenment is the recognition that, in our essence, we are a luminous, breathtaking, glorious, conscious awareness that is not produced by and is not limited to this body-mind. We discover that we are actually not the limited, time-bound creature that we once took ourselves to be. The essence of who and what we are is actually pure God stuff or Buddha stuff. We recognize that we're actually made of a sacred essence or, as the Mahayana Buddhists would say, we have "Buddha nature." Prior to awakening, it seemed that you were this person who was born at a certain time and has lived through certain life experiences and is on a unique journey through this life. And then in an instance of awakening, you realize that who you are is not limited to that little story of self.

You discover: "I am this vast, infinite, sacred consciousness, this immense power, this unstoppable force of love, this care that has no end, this surging well of creativity. I am that, this is who I am." In even a brief moment of awakening, the truth of our divine infinite nature seems so obvious that we find it incomprehensible that we did not see it before. We ask in genuine confusion: "How did I spend my whole life thinking I was something so much smaller and so much more limited than this immensity that is so completely apparent right now and so utterly significant?" Equally astonishing is the simultaneous recognition that all of reality has this same sacred essence. We aren't just awakening to our own essence. We are awakening to the knowledge that all of reality arises from and is permeated with this sacred perfection. The implications of awakening are immense. Although it often initially occurs in fits and starts, when we're finally able to deeply embrace who and what we really are, we become a living expression of this miraculous dimension of being. Our cosmic essence, our super nature, is now free to express itself in this world because we've made room for it, embraced it, and allowed it to come forth. And it changes everything. When we approach meditation as a spiritual practice, we are making a practice out of inviting this profound consciousness to reveal itself within us. We are practicing opening ourselves up to allow awakening to occur. If we can understand the nature of meditation in this way, it will make it much easier to see the ways in which meditation as we may be practicing it might actually be diverting us from this extraordinary possibility.

TWO

THE MYTH OF THE QUIET MIND

What is the greatest obstacle to deep meditation? If you ask a thousand spiritual seekers that question, the vast majority of them will give you some version of the same answer. "It's the mind. It's my busy, relentless mind. I just have so many thoughts. And this seemingly endless stream of thoughts prevents me from really going deep in meditation." I don't know exactly where this rumor got started. But somewhere along the way, nearly all of us learned that meditation is about having a "quiet mind," or eliminating the stream of thoughts, or at least finding a way to focus our mind or make it more "spiritual." And as a result, nearly everyone meditating today is engaged in a misguided—and often exasperating—project of trying to find a way to do something about their active mind. Some of us are trying to get our mind to be quiet. Others are trying to get it to produce more peaceful and spiritual thoughts. And others are trying to find somewhere to place our attention other than our mind—such as our body, or God or our higher self. The idea that meditation is about having a "still" mind is possibly the most pervasive assumption about meditation. Countless people have become frustrated and given up on meditation because they were unable to quiet the mind. But what if I told you the mind wasn't an obstacle to meditation? What if the presence of thoughts had no impact on your ability to meditate at all? As we discussed in Chapter One, meditation in a spiritual context is about the discovery of our true nature. It is a practice designed to open us to enlightened consciousness. So, the question is: what does a quiet mind have to do with enlightened consciousness? To answer this question, imagine what it would be like to go through your entire life without any thoughts. Now, take it a step further and imagine a world in which nobody was thinking anything at all. Ever. It's not a very inspiring picture, is it? If you take it far enough, you end up with the entire human race on intravenous feeding tubes lying there in a vegetative state. Not very enlightened, to say the least. Now imagine an enlightened world—a world in which all human beings are awake to their higher nature, living in awakened consciousness. Clearly it's not a world without thoughts. So is it a world in which everyone only thinks enlightened thoughts? Not exactly. And this brings us back to meditation. Meditation is not about quieting the mind. Nor is it about training the mind to only think good or spiritual thoughts. Meditation, properly understood, is about transforming our relationship to the mind. It's about cultivating the ability to disengage from the mind, to no longer identify with the mind, so that we can discern and discriminate which thoughts are worth listening to and acting on, and which ones aren't. What if you could learn how to not identify with your mind, to not compulsively engage with your thoughts? What if you could learn how, even when there are thoughts present, to not be lost in thoughts, to not mechanically follow the thought stream wherever it goes? Our minds give us trouble because they are deeply conditioned to react in habitual and predictable ways based on past experiences. We're all embedded in countless habits of mind that dictate much of our behavior. Meditation has the potential to liberate you from the mind, which means that no matter how much thought is present, you're not lost in it, you're not compulsively believing it, you're not at the effect of it, you're not afraid of it. Freedom from the mind means freedom in the face of the mind. It doesn't mean freedom from having a mind. It means you are no longer enslaved to your conditioned mind.

So, next time you sit down to meditate, instead of trying to find a way to quiet your mind, simply make the decision to not engage with your mind. That means that when thoughts arise, even if they are very interesting thoughts, we choose not to give them our attention. One of the things that will happen as you meditate in this way is that you'll start to discover that you are not your thoughts, and that you are not even the generator of most of the thoughts you experience. Thoughts just arise spontaneously and somewhat mechanically without any volition on your part. They just keep surfacing; they keep arising on their own. From this vantage point, you begin to see that there is a choice you have, which is to get interested in the content of the thought, to get involved in the thought—or to leave it alone. As you continue with this practice, you eventually come upon a startling discovery—that the content of your mind doesn't need to change in order for you to be able to meditate. In fact, the content of your mind doesn't need to change for you to be awakened. That's because the mind is not the problem. Even having a very active mind is not a problem. In many ways, the power of this practice reveals itself more fully when we have an active mind because it's in those moments that we can begin to discover directly that our true nature is already free even when our mind is in chaos. One of the primary insights of enlightenment is that nothing is an obstacle to our liberation. It doesn't matter if you are in the midst of difficult circumstances, or are experiencing painful emotions, or have a very busy, active mind. You're already free no matter what happens. Consciousness is not at the effect of what arises within it. Who and what you truly are is not governed by the content of your mind from one moment to the next. If you had to have a quiet mind and a peaceful emotional state to be enlightened, I think it's safe to say that nobody would have ever been enlightened in the history of the world. Why?

Because we're human animals with extremely complex brains and deep survival instincts, living active, engaged lives, swept up in a powerful cultural momentum. Our minds are active and reactive in ways that are beyond our control. Spiritual liberation begins to dawn when you discover that your thoughts and feelings have no control over you, that you don't have to believe or even listen to your mind. In that realization, an extraordinary experience of inner freedom begins to emerge out of seemingly nowhere and it changes everything. This inner freedom brings with it numerous remarkable qualities, many of which we'll explore later in this book. But for the purposes of this chapter on the mind, it's worth noting that one of the most noticeable transformations that occurs as we awaken is a profound shift in our way of knowing. The birth of awakened consciousness gives us access to a different kind of knowing than we can access through mere thinking alone. As we continue our practice of being free from the mind, we find that we begin to gain access to a new, holistic "wisdom capacity" that seems to come from beyond what we normally think of as "our mind." This wellspring of spontaneously arising wisdom flows naturally and freely, meeting the needs of each moment with surprising accuracy and clarity. At first, it almost seems like a supernatural ability. But over time, we realize that it is not so much supernatural as it is natural, organic and integrative. It includes our learned knowledge as well as things we never learned. It includes intuition, somatic or bodily knowing as well as "field knowing" or collective wisdom which organically integrates the perspectives of others. It's an integrative, holistic wisdom faculty which doesn't reject thought. It transcends and includes it in a mysterious wider form of knowing that again and again demonstrates its reliability as a profound source of wisdom that we can relax into and trust to guide us. A still mind is something we may experience in moments of meditation, but it's not the ultimate goal, and if we become attached to it, it can even prevent us from discovering meditation's true potential to catalyze spiritual awakening. What is ultimately much more enlightening is learning how to let go of your mind regardless of how active it might be. By doing that, you discover the possibility of being free of your mind no matter what it's doing, which is ultimately much more liberating than merely "shutting it up."

THREE

WHY INNER PEACE IS SO HARD TO FIND

The idea of inner peace has become a kind of holy grail for many spiritual seekers today. Magazine covers and ads feature images of meditators in peaceful natural settings looking serene and unperturbed by the ups and downs of life. And when most of us take up a meditation practice, we do so in a quest to find our own version of that serenity. This is perfectly reasonable. We sense that meditation can bring us more ease, more contentment, more equanimity in the face of life's challenges. And the good news is that it can do all of those things and more. The challenge is that, when most of us envision what inner peace might look like, we imagine ourselves in a tranquil state of perfect emotional contentment in which we feel good, relaxed, and restful—and that everything is as it should be. And, more often than not, we are envisioning that peaceful feeling based on other moments in our lives when we felt really good and content and peaceful inside. So, naturally, we think, "Well, I felt that way before, and I want to feel that way more often. So if I meditate, maybe I can achieve this deep contentment and feel more peaceful all the time." So when we sit down to meditate, we have this picture in our mind, this sort of emotional blueprint of perfect inner peace that we're trying to replicate or recreate—our "inner peace blueprint." And sometimes, we might even succeed in our quest to create that exact feeling of peaceful tranquility. As a spiritual teacher, I often have students who, upon having this experience, will come out of their meditation and report to me with excitement: "Wow, I was really there today, I really got there, I got to that inner peaceful place I'm trying to always get to. It felt so good, I could've stayed there forever." The problem with approaching meditation in this way is that the profound inner peace of genuine enlightenment has very little to do with those feelings of relaxation and tranquility most of us are chasing after and trying to hold on to. And as long as we are using our meditation to try to generate and sustain a peaceful, serene feeling state, we will be missing out on the much more profound opportunity for contentment that meditation can bring to our lives. The contentment that meditation points us toward, the radical inner peace that authentic spiritual practice brings about is a contentment of a completely different order. It's a contentment that is there no matter what we're feeling. It's an equanimity that's there whether we are feeling incredibly upset or angry, deeply sad, ecstatically joyful, bored to tears, or anything else we could possibly feel. The profound contentment of spiritual awakening emerges when we discover a wholeness and fullness of being—an unconditional, uncontainable freedom that is present no matter what's happening. That's the radical possibility of enlightenment, of spiritual transformation. And understanding this can serve as the basis for a very different kind of meditation practice. What would it mean to meditate in a way that was aligned with this profound easefulness, this radical, unconditional contentment? When we realize that meditation is not about achieving a stable feeling of serenity and inner calm, it opens the door to a profound meditation that is not about trying to catalyze any particular feeling state. In this practice, we make room for any and all feeling experiences to come and go during our meditation, without preference or resistance. This practice of radical contentment is not about relaxing your mind or your body; nor is it about getting rid of any and all emotional reactivity. The ease and contentment that spiritual awakening points us to is about being at ease no matter what we're experiencing. It's about finding a part of yourself that is already deeply content with what is, even when you have a busy, active mind, even when you're feeling a lot of emotional reactivity going on, even when there's physical tension in the body.Practicing resting in this fundamental contentment means making room for everything that could possibly happen in your meditation. This means that even if your mind seems to be a "monkey mind" generating disturbing thoughts, or you're feeling emotional tension about something happening in your life, you're practicing being at ease in the face of all of it. I'll be the first to acknowledge that what I'm pointing to is an utterly radical proposition. Indeed, this practice runs counter to just about every human instinct we have. You may find it inconceivable to simply be at ease no matter what you're feeling, no matter what your mind is doing, no matter what your body feels, to just be utterly content and at ease and have no problem with any of it. But I would suggest that it only seems preposterous because we have been taught to think of being content or at ease as an emotional state. In the way we normally speak about inner peace and contentment, we mean being emotionally content, or feeling peaceful. But spiritual awakening is not about being emotionally content. It's much deeper than that. It's about being existentially content. It means you are content at the deepest level of your being. You are content with existence as it is, without prejudice. One of the simplest ways to practice this ultimate contentment is to just refuse to make a problem out of anything that happens during your meditation. When we do this, we usually pretty quickly start to notice our lack of contentment. We start to notice all the subtle ways that we're not quite right with reality, that we're not quite content with what is, that we're not quite sure that we're okay with what's happening. And that's what this practice is designed to get up underneath and, ultimately, turn on its head—this fundamental existential discontent or angst which is almost always the substrate of human experience. It's almost always there, under the surface, in the background, driving our choices in life. This sense that there's not enough, "I'm not enough, life is not enough, this moment is not enough yet." The good news is that a peaceful meditation is not the holy grail. Something much bigger—and more profound—is possible through meditation. What's possible is the cultivation of steadiness in the face of every changing life experience. This heightened capacity is much more significant than any superficial and fleeting "peace" that may or may not occur in meditation. It's a kind of calm that is deeper and more enduring. Fully embraced, it is nothing less than liberation itself. Imagine the freedom in remaining consistent no matter how difficult or uncomfortable circumstances become—a relationship to your feelings that is unconditional. That's one result this meditation can bring about—and it has very little to do with feeling good during the meditation.

FOUR

THE MISGUIDED QUEST FOR PEAK EXPERIENCES

In the previous chapter, we discussed how the quest for a feeling of inner peace can block us from discovering the profound potential of meditation. In this chapter, we look at a similar meditation detour—the quest for "peak experiences" during meditation. Many of us come to meditation practice because we've read or heard about extraordinary experiences of spiritual enlightenment that meditation can help bring about. Depending on our background, we may meditate with the expectation that it will release powerful experiences of spiritual energy, open us to overwhelming spiritual bliss and joy, or reveal an earthshattering spiritual insight or satori. And, through our engagement with meditation and other spiritual practices, many of us have had these and other powerful experiences. But whether we've only read about them in books or experienced them directly for ourselves, peak experiences can be a trap for any of us on the spiritual path—particularly if we mistake these experiences for the true goal of enlightenment. When I speak about peak experiences, I want to acknowledge that there are hundreds – possibly thousands – of different types of spiritual experiences that meditation can bring about. We can have experiences of oneness, in which we feel like we have merged with everything in the universe and lose the ability to distinguish between our self and everything else. We can experience powerful spiritual feelings of bliss or ecstasy that overwhelms our system. We can have experiences where we feel and see the interconnectedness of everything–that everything touches and influences everything else and that nothing has an independent existence. We can have spiritual experiences where we're overcome with awe and reverence for the sacred. We can have spiritual experiences with another person – a feeling of like a deep soul connection with another, where we feel our consciousness becomes one. We can have experiences of merging with the natural world – of union with nature. We can have experiences of divine love, in which we realize that we are loved or that our nature is love and that love is always here, ever present, always flowing. We can have spiritual experiences of intense clarity in which everything becomes lucid and crystal and clear. We can have experiences of intense powerful energy. We can have spiritual experiences of a kind of expansiveness and openness – a boundlessness where all the boundaries dissolve and there's just this kind of infinite space. And we can have hundreds, if not thousands, of other kinds of spiritual experiences as well. These are all wonderful experiences to have. Peak experiences are often transformational because of what they reveal to us. They also often give us powerful motivation to pursue the spiritual path. When we have these experiences, we feel temporarily connected to a much greater reality and this can build our faith and compel us to be more wholehearted in our spiritual practice. So, what could possibly be wrong with peak experiences? Nothing whatsoever. The problem only arises when we mistake these experiences with the goal of the spiritual path. (Which, by the way, almost everyone does). Because once we make this mistake, we can't help but come to meditation seeking after a special experience. When we think about the goal of the spiritual path, most of us imagine ourselves permanently elevated into some kind of higher state of consciousness. Whether it's an ongoing experience of deep inner peace, expansive freedom, boundless inspiration or remarkable clarity of mind, most of us find it hard to conceive of spiritual awakening as anything other than a profound transformation of our consciousness. As a result, most meditators are, consciously or unconsciously, seeking after a specific feeling state or experience that they assume is the goal of meditation. We may pursue this higher state of consciousness during the meditation, or as a result of the meditation—or both.

It's perfectly natural to assume that reaching "the right state of consciousness" is the goal and the answer to an enlightened life. That's because at first glance, we can see that when we're experiencing these higher states, we tend to behave in more enlightened ways. When we feel good, we tend to have more perspective, be more caring, and navigate challenges more easily. Simply, we notice that when we feel good, it's easier to show up as our highest self. Observing this connection, we then assume that those feelings are the cause of our best behavior. We figure those feelings have to be in place first if we want to show up in an empowered, enlightened manner. And so most of our spiritual and personal growth effort is devoted to trying to reach — and then forever maintain — these "ideal" states. The problem with seeking after peak experiences is that these powerful states inevitably come and go. Any emotional quality or higher state we can experience will always be fleeting. Meditative states, like any other state of consciousness, are inherently transitory, passing states. The nature of feelings is that they always change in response to what life brings our way. Sometimes we experience anger because something frustrating or unjust happened in the world. Sometimes we experience joy because something wonderful happened. Sometimes we experience peace and contentment either because something good happened or maybe, for a brief period, nothing happened, and we were able to just relax. But all of these are just temporary, passing states of consciousness. Experiences in meditation, no matter how profound they might seem, are fundamentally no different. Peak experiences don't really have anything to do with the point of meditation or the point of spiritual awakening, even if they're nice feelings and experiences to have. Even if we go away to a retreat or workshop and experience the most exalted state we've ever known — and it seems like we'll never touch down — when we get back into the complex realities of our daily life, our state of consciousness will inevitably change once again. That's simply the nature of being human. If you achieve a "desired" state briefly, you may be disappointed when it inevitably passes or "crashes." Then you might conclude that the meditation didn't work. Even if we weren't initially looking for a peak experience in our meditation, many people who do have a special experience during meditation get fixated on trying to recreate that experience—especially if the heightened state is particularly exciting. Inevitably, when we try to permanently "lock in" or reproduce our higher states, we're disappointed. We may think we've "failed" in our aspirations to evolve. We wonder why we're not "getting there." It even begins to seem as if true enlightenment is a distant or perhaps impossible goal. Achieving a higher state of consciousness is not the point of meditation, and it's actually counterproductive to its real purpose. Trying to achieve a higher state permanently is doomed to fail—but more importantly, it isn't even necessary or desirable. Meditation is about the practice of liberation from all states—an equal relationship to everything that arises or ever could arise. Rather than pursuing a special state of consciousness, when we meditate, we're seeking to discover the enlightened, liberated consciousness that's always already here no matter what experience we're having. We're learning how to bring our attention and our presence to the extraordinary consciousness that is already here reading these words right now and looking out of your eyes right now. We're endeavoring to discover that this sacred consciousness is always here right now in the midst of everything else that's here right now. We're not trying to get to a special place other than right here which we discover to our amazement is always an incredibly special place when we stop trying to get somewhere else.

FIVE

AVOID FALLING INTO A MEDITATION RUT

one of the biggest challenges meditators consistently report is that their meditation practice has become repetitive, monotonous and even dull. By its nature, meditation is designed to bring us into contact with the dynamic aliveness of our own true nature. Ideally, it should give us a potent sense of always being poised just "on the edge" of the unknown. Yet, all too often, I hear from people who have been meditating for years that when they first started meditating, their practice was vibrant and alive with possibility, but now, many years later, they feel like that spiritual potency they once felt has been lost and they are simply "going through the motions" with their practice. They may feel more calm and centered as a result of their years of practice. But the fire of spiritual awakening that once compelled them to meditate has been replaced by a sense that they "should" meditate because "it's good for them." It's important to realize that this sense of monotony isn't our fault. Most of us who have been taught traditional meditation practices have been encouraged to take up a single meditation technique and repeat it over and over every day for years or even decades. There are and always have been good reasons for this repetitive approach. We all know that practice makes perfect and that a certain amount of repetition is required to become proficient at anything— including meditation. Yet while commitment and consistency are essential, simply repeating the same practice can cause your meditation to quickly lose its vitality and dynamism. Meditation for your mind and spirit is in some ways like exercise for the body. If you perform the same exercise repeatedly at the same level, it will cease to challenge you or produce results. Doing the identical meditation every day for years on end can be like taking the same daily walk at the same pace. It can become unsatisfying and also hold you back from the new and deeper places you could go by stretching yourself. While in essence all forms of meditation are like spokes on a wheel, "pointing to the same place," it is only by incorporating a variety of different approaches that we can cultivate a range of capacities that strengthen our ability to open to meditative depth. And because we all process differently and are at different points on the path, it's normal for some approaches to feel more accessible than others. Experimenting with different gateways into the depths of meditation is part of what supports us to forge a deeply fulfilling relationship with our practice. Even if you've found a particular practice that really speaks to you, by "cross training" with practices that are more challenging, you can broaden and deepen your understanding of meditation's goal, which often leads to new insights. As your practice continues to evolve, variation and novelty also become increasingly important antidotes to the natural tendency for your mind to become too involved in the process. This happens when a practice is familiar and you start to think you know "how to do it," and begin developing internal reference points or expectations for how the meditation should unfold. The practice quickly starts to feel flat and boring, because on some level, you already think you know what is going to happen. The lively, mysterious dimension at the heart of meditation has slipped out of reach. By experimenting with new and unfamiliar practices, we can cultivate our ability to remain curious, and curiosity is what sharpens our awareness and keeps us always on the edge of our own understanding. This is why I encourage an approach to meditation that always includes a balance of newness and variation. When you "cross-train" your meditative mind, you can create a meditation practice that truly feels like an adventure because it is always leading you forward into the unknown. You'll find that this approach eliminates the potential for getting "stuck in a rut," and turns your meditation practice into an ongoing journey of deepening awakeness and curiosity. Truly, there is no end to where you can go with this kind of meditation.

SIX

THE TRAP OF PRACTICING WITH A FUTURE GOAL IN MIND

The last meditation mistake I want to discuss isn't so much an error in how we're practicing, but a confusion in how we're approaching the whole endeavor of meditation. When we think about meditation practice, almost invariably, we think about it as a process that occurs over a period of time. We envision a future goal that we imagine meditation will help to bring about, and then we take up a practice which we imagine will gradually move us closer to that goal. We've heard that if we meditate for 20 or 30 minutes a day, a number of good things might happen for us. Our stress levels might come down. We might become more focused and attentive. We might become happier. We might experience more joy. We might be able to focus better and be more present and attentive. We're doing our practice now in the hope that these good things will come from it in the future. Others of us take up meditation in pursuit of enlightenment or spiritual awakening. We start doing these practices now in the hope that sometime in the future we'll have an experience of spiritual illumination. We'll become enlightened. So, in this case, we're practicing as preparation for awakening, or to add momentum to our potential for awakening. It's as though, every time we practice, we imagine we're putting a little gas in the tank of the engine of awakening. And we assume that if we just do enough of it long enough, then maybe that extraordinary, mysterious event will happen and hopefully happen in a way that is able to be sustained, not just in a flash, but in a way that's enduring. At first glance, this goal orientation seems to make sense. After all, this is how we've been taught to relate to any goal we might pursue. And it's how we've accomplished probably everything else we've achieved in our life. But when it comes to meditation and spiritual awakening, this future orientation is actually a major hindrance on the path. As long as it's in place, it will likely prevent us from discovering the true magic of meditation and the mystery of awakened consciousness.Spiritual traditions ancient and modern have always asserted that spiritual awakening is about the discovery of a sacred dimension of reality and a sacred dimension of ourselves that already exists right now, complete and whole. And, anyone who has even a glimpse of awakening realizes that it is only about discovering the sacredness and wholeness of this moment right now, and that any investment in a future moment of enlightenment is missing the entire point. The simple, paradigm-shattering truth of enlightenment is that it can only ever be discovered right now in this moment. Any belief that we could do something now to prepare us for a future awakening will always be an obstacle to the immediate realization of enlightenment here and now. Indeed, some spiritual teachers have gone so far as to discourage any form of spiritual practice, asserting that the very idea of "practice" is a postponement of our enlightenment, a denial of the fact that our true self is already enlightened. And while I don't agree that spiritual practice itself should be left behind, I do agree that meditating as a means to get to a future goal of enlightenment will never achieve its intended result. In order to unlock the power of meditation, it is imperative that we find a way to practice that brings the goal fully into the present moment. The paradigm shift I'm pointing to is so significant that, for most of us, it will seem impossibly paradoxical. But there is a way to do it. It's what I call "the practice of direct awakening." And it is to this whole new way of looking at meditation practice that we will now turn our attention.

SEVEN

THE PRACTICE OF DIRECT AWAKENING

Genuine spiritual awakening has always been the pinnacle of human aspiration. If you've had even a glimpse of this profound spiritual potential, you know that an extraordinary, enlightened life is possible–a life filled with meaning and purpose, in which you have access to a seemingly limitless well of inspiration, wisdom, love and creativity. So, why is that, for thousands of years, the supreme goal of Enlightenment has been shrouded in mystery, believed to be accessible only indirectly through decades (or even lifetimes) of repetitive and often tedious meditation practice? As a spiritual practitioner, it never made sense to me that spiritual awakening should be so inaccessible. After all, spiritual masters East and West have always told us that the miracle of Enlightened Consciousness already exists, fully formed, inside of each of us–that this luminous awareness is none other than our own true nature. If this awakened "spiritual nature" is truly who we already are, why would it be nearly impossible to gain consistent, ongoing access to it? It was my pursuit of this inquiry over decades of spiritual practice and teaching that eventually led me to a discovery that turned my entire world upside down. The context for the inquiry that gave birth to the Practice of Direct Awakening was a series of evolutionary laboratories I had the good fortune to participate in. When I talk about an evolutionary laboratory, I'm not referring to a sterile environment where people in lab coats attach electrodes to the scalps of meditators. I'm referring to a place where dedicated spiritual practitioners come together and spend thousands of hours doing spiritual practice and experimenting with awakening. It was in one such laboratory that this new way of approaching meditation and spiritual enlightenment emerged. The radical discovery that completely transformed my understanding of spiritual awakening is that it is possible to meditate in such a way that enables us to tap directly into the infinite energy, intelligence and freedom of enlightenment every time we practice. Instead of doing practices designed to bring about a future moment of awakening, we simply need to learn how to practice "being awake" right now. It's a subtle shift in approach. But it changes everything. In order to begin this exploration of the approach to meditation I call "the practice of direct awakening," I want to invite you to temporarily set aside everything you've already learned about meditation. Not because I think what you've learned is wrong or that this approach is "better," but simply because the approach to meditation I'm describing may have little or nothing in common with meditation as you've been practicing it—other than the outer posture of sitting still for a while every day. For most of us, meditating means silently repeating a mantra or sacred word, or following our breath, or labeling our thoughts and feelings as they arise, or trying to become a witness of our mind. But this practice is about something entirely different. It is a practice of directly recognizing our Enlightened essence or what is often referred to as "awakened awareness" or "awakened consciousness." In other words, the Practice of Direct Awakening is an approach to meditation designed to bring us into the immediate and direct awareness of our true nature beyond the mind and ego. It is not a practice we do now to prepare for a future moment of Enlightenment.It is not a practice we do now in order to get better at something or to strengthen particular capacities. It is a practice of being Awake right now. Of being Enlightened right now. This is possible because Enlightenment is the discovery of who we already are. It is the discovery of our "true nature." The revolutionary proposition at the heart of the Practice of Direct Awakening is that we don't have to wait for Awakening to happen to us. We don't have to spend a lifetime practicing various techniques in the hope that one day we will stumble upon awakened consciousness. It's possible to actually practice being Awake, or resting in our true nature which is always already Awake. At the heart of this paradigm shift is the recognition that just as our ordinary, unawakened consciousness operates in predictable ways, awakened consciousness also functions in reliable, observable ways. And if we can observe and understand how the natural functioning of awakened consciousness works, we can learn how to practice stepping directly into it. For instance, if you've ever had a moment of awakening, you probably noticed that awakened consciousness is fluid, flexible, open and at ease. It does not grasp after certainty. It does not identify with thoughts and feelings. It does not react mechanically to circumstances. And it is naturally aware of the vast open field of consciousness itself. When we engage in The Practice of Direct Awakening, we practice all of these things in meditation. We practice letting go. We practice letting things be. We practice not clinging on to the mind, not grasping after certainty and not identifying with thought. We practice simply being present, awake, and aware and not in reaction to what's happening. We practice not holding out for a better future, not looking for enlightenment or fulfillment somewhere other than in this moment.

All of these and many other natural attitudes or dispositions of awakening are things that you and I can sit down for 30 minutes a day and practice. When we do this, we're practicing relating to our minds, our feelings, and this world in an enlightened way. Instead of waiting for enlightenment to happen to us, we're practicing being enlightened. Instead of waiting to wake up, we're practicing being awake. Instead *of waiting for a spiritual explosion to break us out of the prison of the ego, we're practicing being free in each moment. Another way to look at this is that when we do The Practice of Direct Awakening, we're creating daily opportunities for awakened consciousness to show up by practicing a way of being that only awakened consciousness can participate in. Your ego can't do any of the practices I just described. But you can. And when you do, you're making room for a profound mystery, an infinite dimension of being, to show up in your experience right now. What if awakening didn't have to be a long, drawn-out process leading toward an ultimately unpredictable result? What if, instead of spending the next 10, 20, or 30 years doing mindfulness practices, watching your breath or repeating mantras in an attempt to prepare for Enlightenment, you could engage in a daily practice that gave you direct access to Awakened Consciousness right now? What if, instead of hoping for a lightning bolt of spiritual insight to awaken you sometime in the distant future, you could practice aligning with the limitless energy, intelligence and freedom of Enlightenment every single day? If you've been struggling with meditation and other practices for any length of time, you may find that what I'm asserting sounds just too good to be true, or too easy to be genuinely transformational.*

But, after teaching the Practice of Direct Awakening to thousands of people over the past decade, I can say with confidence that anybody with a sincere aspiration to Awaken can do this. You can do this. It doesn't have to take a lifetime to wake up.

EIGHT

OPENING TO THE MIRACLE OF AWAKENED AWARENESS

As a teacher of Direct Awakening, one of the questions I hear most often is: "Is Enlightenment really possible?" Of course, it doesn't always come phrased in such simple terms. But, however it is expressed, the question so many of us are asking is: "Can I really elevate my consciousness and my life into a consistent, sustained expression of the profound depth I've glimpsed in my most sacred moments?" Is it possible, in other words, to be truly free, unconditionally awake to the sacred depth that is our own true nature beyond the mind and ego? When we started out on the spiritual path, most of us had a sense that an extraordinary spiritual transformation was possible—a radical realignment at the deepest levels of our being that would not only liberate us from personal suffering but would infuse our life with a sacred, cosmic sense of meaning, purpose and wholeness. Yet after years or even decades of working on ourselves, many of us have begun to doubt whether that initial intuition of our higher potential was more fantasy than reality. My hope is that what I've

shared in this short book will give you faith that the highest possibility you've glimpsed, the most glorious potential you've sensed, is not a figment of your imagination but a real, living possibility. And that even more than that is possible. It is possible for life to make perfect sense. It's possible for YOUR life to make perfect sense. It's possible to come into such profound alignment with the moral and spiritual axis of the cosmos that every moment of your life is a walk in grace, and a living demonstration of the mysterious, inherent goodness of the life process itself.It's possible to awaken so deeply to the sacred evolutionary impulse at the heart of existence that our words, actions and choices become a dynamic expression of the highest possibility there is. And in this transformation, it's possible to discover an unimaginable and abiding liberation from the suffering of the confused, neurotic, separate sense of self. It's possible, in other words, to be truly free. What I'm speaking about is a completely different kind of human life than most of us have ever encountered. This is not simply about "being in the now" or "loving and accepting what is in every moment." It is not about simply accessing a more expansive state of awareness or being able to stand back and abide as the "witness" of all that arises. All of these are good experiences to have and important capacities to cultivate. But I'm speaking about something more. I'm pointing to authentic spiritual awakening in which the ego has been radically overridden by the Ultimate principle, by the creative force of the cosmos, by what the Buddha called "the roar of the timeless beyond." It's a life in which our endless quest for self-fulfillment has been replaced by a passion to give everything to bringing our life into alignment with the sacred perfection we've discovered in our deepest moments. In this ultimate submission to and alignment with the Absolute, we become a living, breathing force for higher evolution and awakening. This changes our relationship to being alive in unimaginable ways. Experientially, we find ourself in a state of profound receptivity and openness. A deep and abiding simplicity pervades our life, and an ongoing sense of flow permeates every moment. We have let go of identification with the mind and abandoned any attachment to the self, enabling us to live as a transparent, vibrant vessel for the Infinite. Amidst this profound openness, there is remarkable mental clarity at times, but there is no clinging on to that clarity. Insights come and go, but there is the knowledge that "I can't hold onto any of this," and so there is no grasping onto certainty. Yet in moments when clarity is needed, it miraculously appears, integrating all of our knowledge and lived experience in a flash of intuitive knowing. Spiritual experiences come and go, too, but there is no longer any clinging to ecstasy, bliss or love. We have discovered the source of all these things, and so feel no compulsion to cling to them. More importantly, and contrary to popular belief, we awaken to a profound awareness of what we might call the heart of the cosmos. We feel, in a sense, for the Whole of Life. We feel the pain of the whole and the joy of the whole as our own pain and our own joy. We become a seeing, sensing, feeling organ of Reality itself. We also find that, because we are no longer obstructing the infinite power and depth of awakened consciousness, many of the capacities and qualities we've been trying to cultivate in ourselves are suddenly available to us without effort. We find that we're filled with a dynamic source of energy that is seemingly limitless—energy to do whatever needs to be done in each moment. This energy is no longer coming from our body, but from somewhere mysterious that we can't see. We also find we can tap into a seemingly infinite well of creativity, as though the creative power of the cosmos is coursing through us. Whenever we need it, it is available. We discover we also have access to a wellspring of inner strength that gives us steadiness and confidence in the face of life's challenges. No matter what life throws our way, we're not daunted. We have a fundamental trust that we'll find our way, that the resources needed to meet life's demands will appear. From where, we don't know, but we trust that they will, and we find that they do. I'm not talking about trusting that an all powerful God or "universe" is going to take care of us, or that mystical things will happen in our life to make everything work. Instead, there's a kind of trust in an inner resource that is always readily available to us. We also find an unprecedented ability to be present in a way that most of us have never experienced. And in this powerful presence, we become a finely tuned receptive instrument that can sense into the deeper needs and feelings of those around us, and into what we might call the evolutionary needs of the moment. We can feel it with our being. And this enables us spontaneously discern the path of positive action in a way that transcends mere cognition. And at the center of our being is a burning passion for evolution and transformation, a calling to transform the world into an expression of the great perfection we have discovered to be its source. All of this may sound very lofty and beyond reach, but I want to make it clear that this is not a pipe dream drawn from ancient books. This is a real and living possibility for each of us. This is what human life—your life—can become. The game-changing discovery behind the Practice of Direct Awakening is that there is a deeper "essential supernature" that already exists within each of us fully formed.

This "essential supernature" already contains the extraordinary capacities that most of us are striving to develop. And now, instead of spending decades doing "indirect" practices to try to develop all of these abilities one at a time, we can literally practice tapping directly into the source of these capacities every single day